52

BY

DANNY STRACK

WWW.DANNYSTRACK.COM

MAP OF THE INTERNET [1]

[1] *2014 Map of the Internet created using data from* *http://internet-map.net/*

This book is filled with similar footnote hyperlinks!

In most cases, these links aren't source material,
but rather resources and references to learn more about the topics.

All graphs, diagrams and drawings are original creations of Dny,
with data sources appropriately listed in the footnotes.

DEDICATED TO:
THE INTERNET

Thank you for so much information.
I only hope I can turn it into wisdom.

Also for my family:
Carm, Dick, Eddy, Julie, Juliana, Krystal, Mike, Nikki, Penny (the Wise), Penny (the Young), Vic, all Sabins, all Stracks, the whole Saratoga NY Clan, Chris G, Jean K & Kristina H, Kimily K.W., Rebecca T, Thomas G, and Winnie H.

Endless thanks to the entire Texas spoken word community, specifically the poets of Austin Slam, Austin Neo-Soul, Spider House, Spitshine, Austin They Speak, AIPF, Spoken & Heard, Mic Check, Houston VIP, Write About Now, Puroslam, DPS, Inkwell, KPS, Corpus Christi ¡Ballabajoomba! Slam, El Paso Free Hole Slam, Slamarillo, & Laredo Border Slam, and I really do mean every single member of our poetry family.

Bonus thanks to Andy, Anna, Anastacio, Anthony, Ariana, B-Fran, BPE, Bean, Bill, Brently, Charles, Chibbi, Chris, Christopher, Da'Shade, Danielle, David, Davis, Desireé, Digg, Ebony, Edwin, Eric, Faylita, Gabrielle, Glori, Greta, Herman, Jacob, Jess, Jo, Joe, John, Jomar, Joshua, Julian, Keith, Kevin, Korim, Krissi, Lacey, Lance, Love, Maddie, MRO, MetraNohm, MJC, Mike, Olivia, Peter, Phil, Ron, Rooster, Rayner, Sabrina, Safi, Sarah, Seth, Shae, Shaggy, Shannon, Shelia, Stefan, Tony, Tova, Vicki, Zachary, Zai, and the rest of the slam teams, councils & crews that currently (or formerly) run stuff in Texas & beyond. This book wouldn't exist without you.

Extra special thanks to Barb I, Robby C, Ruff Draft, & Sacha J, for edits, feedback and other contributions throughout the book.

MAP OF CONTENTS

GREATEST IN THE WORLD ~ P. 26

HITLARITY ~ P. 24

2 OUT OF 5 ~ P. 22

AT THAT MOMENT, I REALIZED I'M WEIRD ~ P. 20

MARKETING MYSELF ~ P. 18

DENIM, DENIM, DENIM ~ P. 16

PORNOGRAPHY DRIVES INNOVATION ~ P. 14

THE INTERNET IS NOT FOR STUPID SHARKS ~ P. 12

ZOOM OUT ~ P. 9

CLICK HERE ~ P. 6

MAP OF CONTENTS ~ P.3
(YOU ARE HERE)

WHIRRRRRRR KA'CHING ~ P. 29

WHISTLEBLOWERS ~ P. 30

CORPORATIONS ARE PEOPLE ~ P. 32

OPEN LETTER TO MY UNBORN GRANDCHILDREN ~ P. 34

TALK TO YOUR KIDS ABOUT LOVE ~ P. 36

STARK ~ P. 38

SWIM OR TAKE A BOAT ~ P. 40

PAPER ~ P. 42

BINARY BRAIN ~ P. 43

DIAGRAM OF NEUROANATOMY VERSUS TECHNOLOGY ~ P. 46

THIS IS GONNA HURT ~ P. 48

ABOUT DNY ~ P. 52

CLICK HERE

Buy Shoes. Nike. Red.
Click

Cheap! Green swoosh. Perfect for Christmas.
To purchase, click here.
Click

Thanks! If you'd like to learn more about shoes, click here.
Click [1]

For every fifty shoes sold in our country,
forty-nine were made overseas,
just like your clothes, phone and everything else you own,
most of our stuff is manufactured in sweatshops.

If you'd like to learn more about the low-cost workers, click here.
Click. [2]

Right now, it is 6 A.M. in Moscow and 11 A.M. in Seoul.
All across Asia, over a billion women and children are starting a twelve-hour workday.
They will be paid pennies to pack, press, process, clean, carry, sew.
They are shrinking from malnutrition and toxic conditions.
Shrinking like Christmas elves who cobble together your shoes for crumbs overnight and disappear in the morning.
You never see them.

Even as aid organizations crack down in one country,
the corporations that own the elves are growing...
in every other country on Earth.
God, how do we still have hells like these in America? [3]

Meanwhile, the companies bribe up influence everywhere,
shattering economic and ecosystems in each region they enter.

If you'd like to learn more about instability, click here.
Click

God help you if you were born poor in this world.
May God and science work together to help you if you were denied guidance and a chance to go to school.
If your parents sold you into slavery.
If your only options were sweatshop or sexshop.

If you'd like to hear the children's voices, click here.
...
If you'd like to see their faces, click here.
...
If you want to do something about it, click here.
Click

If you want to donate all your money to charity, click here.
Click

Thanks! Your generous five thousand dollar donation made up zero point zero, zero, zero, zero, zero, four percent of the leading aid organization's revenue this year.
You just bought one-tenth of a plate at one top-donor campaign dinner,
a Band-Aid for a gangrenous leg wound,
a drop in a silo of AIDS medicine that will be mishandled and misappropriated by local militias.

If you'd like to learn more about your inability to help, click here.
Click

We keep electing the same politicians sewn into the pockets of the sweatshop corporations, but your vote doesn't matter 'cause only the rich have enough free speech cash to make their voice heard...
and if money is speech then speech is not free.

This is the economics of inequality,
not just in America, but everywhere.

If you'd like to learn more about campaign finance reform, voting district gerrymandering, foreign aid mismanagement, vertical corporate integration, and rampant cronyism designed to keep power in the hands of the rich, click here.
Click

Chase the rabbit down the hole far enough,
we thought we'd find wonderland,
and everything we ever wanted,
but instead we find no bottom.
Just a world wide web, and we're all wrapped up.

And the giant spider is eating the rabbit.
Our hubris eating our greed.
And God, we love shoes.

If you'd like to learn more about spiders,
click here.

---

[1] *http://www.businessinsider.com/how-nike-changed-the-shoe-industry-2014-4*
[2] *http://www.laborrights.org/industries/apparel*
[3] *https://www.dosomething.org/facts/11-facts-about-sweatshops*

ZOOM OUT

Epidemiologists track the spread of disease on maps using points and lines. [1]

Every infected person is a point, linked to other people-points by lines showing the transmission of the sickness:

Fred gave the flu to Sue, who passed it to Betty and you.

Zoom Out
...from where you stand and watch the world curve out from under you like the surface of a skull. See the motherboard cities of people splayed across the continents. See their spindly connections shine!

Zoom In
Sociologists adapted the same model to track the spread of ideas.
Ideas are infectious, every enlightened person a point:

Fred taught philosophy to Sue, who passed it to Betty and you.

The better the concept, the more contagious.
That's what it really means to go viral.

Zoom Out
...and picture history. See the map snowflakes sparkle as we develop!
Follow the idea of heaven, reincarnation, nirvana.
Track the transmission of capitalism, racism, of every ism there ever was.
See the golden rule spin through each vector!

Zoom In
Epidemiologists and Sociologists use the concept of a 'super-spreader' to identify a point with lots of connections. [2]

If you have gonorrhea and tons of unprotected sex,
you are a super-spreader of the clap.

If there was an outbreak in Austin,
transmission lines would vector off you in every direction.
Epidemiologists wish you used a condom.

Zoom Out
...and see small ideas grow into big ones.
Blacksmiths forge ahead through iron to steel, electricity explained, computers created, scores of scientists turn around the internet.
Now we have the data and technology to build epidemiological tracking maps like the ones I'm talking about in this poem!
You could use one to track everyone who ever watched Gangnam Style,
or the spread and subversion of the Harlem Shake. [3]

Zoom In
If anyone taught you anything today,
you've been infected with a new idea.

Zoom Out
...and find yourself.
Who are you connected to?
Who do you influence?
Who influences you?

Zoom In
Authors, celebrities, public personalities, poets and politicians, anyone with a podium or a YouTube channel,
you are the super-spreaders of notions, theories and thoughts.

If you're going to spread ideas,
make sure they aren't the conceptual equivalent of the clap.

Zoom Out
...can you see the harp strings between us right now?
What would happen if I strummed them?

Zoom In
Now put on your most infectious smile.

Zoom Out
...can you see <u>your</u> influence?

---

[1] *http://en.wikipedia.org/wiki/Graph_theory#Applications*
[2] *http://en.wikipedia.org/wiki/Super-spreader*
[3] *http://en.wikipedia.org/wiki/Harlem_Shake_(meme)#Viral_spread*

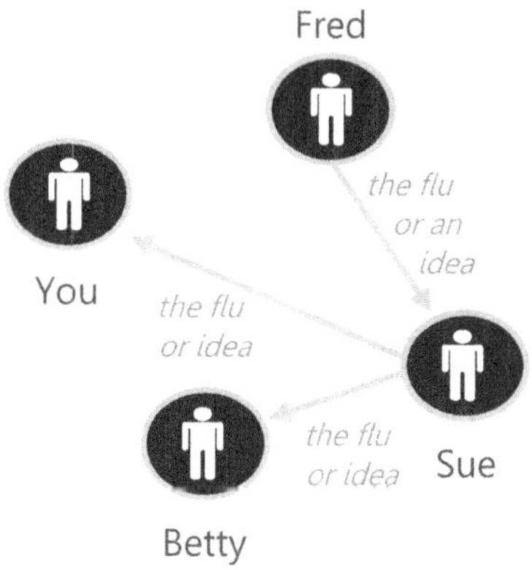

—Figure 1—

Points and lines represent the movement of diseases and/or ideas across a network of people.

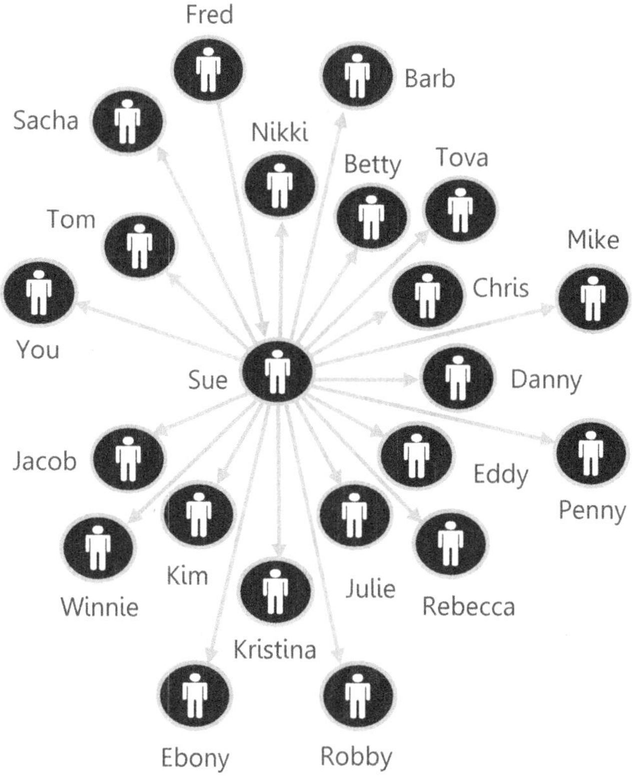

—Figure 2—

Sue is a super-spreader.

THE INTERNET IS NOT FOR STUPID SHARKS

It......used......ta......beee...ee...ee...ee...
Click. [Pause].
Buffering, buffering, buffering...
buffering, buffering, buffering...
buffering, buffering, buffering... [1]
Click.
...that if you were having a conversation with some dumb person or some dumb shark, and the shark said something stupid like,

"Did you know that Madonna won the Grammy for Video of the Year in 1984 for the song "Physical?""

And you said,
"I don't think that's true. And I would know!"

You could end up arguing about that crap all night, till you get really frustrated and you grab the shark by its stupid shark throat, and scream, *"Stupid shark! You're full of fish!"* [2]

The next thing you know, you're having shark tacos for breakfast.

But now you don't have to do that anymore.
You can just turn to the repository of all accumulated human knowledge, and Bing that thing!

Bing! Wiki-wiki-wiki!

Madonna didn't sing "Physical!" It was Olivia Newton John! And she won that Grammy in 1983, the last year that they awarded it! [3]
You FAIL stupid shark!
You'd know that if sharks had developed the internet.

But you didn't. [4]

Meanwhile, the Internet is the sickest, most epic WIN in the history of mankind!

The internet has everything from cats to porn,
and soon it's gonna have both at the same time!

I'm starting a new site with videos of cats having sex,
but I can't decide what to call it, pussypussy.com or kittieporn.com.
And it's not bestiality if there's no human's involved, right?
The internet says that's right! [5]

Know what else Wikipedia says about animals and penetration?
Almost all non-mammalian species, we're talking reptiles, birds,
amphibians... stupid sharks... only have one hole in their posterior
called a 'cloaca', and with their cloaca, they excrete urine and feces...
and have sex! [6]

Where else are you going to hear about that?

Another win for the internet!

So the next time you hear some stupid shark saying something stupid,
You can just smack it and say,
"shut.......your......teeth ... hole......."

Click. [Pause].
Buffering, buffering, buffering...
buffering, buffering, buffering...
Click.

"...or I just might have to get Madonna to get physical on that cloaca!
Stupid shark!"

---

1 https://en.wikipedia.org/wiki/Data_buffer
2 https://en.wikipedia.org/wiki/Shark#Feeding
3 https://en.wikipedia.org/wiki/Olivia_Physical
4 https://en.wikipedia.org/wiki/History_of_the_Internet
5 https://en.wikipedia.org/wiki/Zoophilia
6 https://en.wikipedia.org/wiki/Cloaca

PORNOGRAPHY DRIVES INNOVATION

"Og?"

"Guh?"

"Me like ladies."

"Mmmmm."

"Here. You take mammoth tusk.
Carve lady shape."

"Mmmm. Good idea. You smart, Guh."

And so, porn was born!
Forty thousand years ago.
Did you know,
the oldest statue of a person ever found, is a round naked female form?

And most folks don't think this is porn.
These Venus figurines are symbols of fertility.

And I agree...
But what exactly does that mean?
And even if they were carved by caveladies to celebrate fertility...
Can you think of any other uses her caveman compatriots might have made with with the busty statuettes later in the evening after the ceremonies and caveladies went to bed?

If it weren't for porn, we might not have art at all!

They drew naked ladies on every wall!
The first cave paintings were of man's downfall.

Fast forward to the future, we're still obsessed,
with drawings and video of women undressed.

It killed Betamax for the VHS,
and now it drives the internets!

Every technological pinnacle we've ever hit, is instantly taken over by pictures of tits, and then driven and strengthened by this.

From the VCRs to DVDs,
to the bandwidth we need for streaming movies.

And you can bet, when they perfect
perfect virtual reality,
with full tactile response, plus olfactory,
it will be so that we can have sex with alien mermaid celebrities.

Love it or leave it, but you have to agree,
porno drives artistic innovation and technology! [1]

HAIKU

Tried to circle jerk with my best friend,
but could only line segment jerk.

[1] http://www.businessinsider.com/how-porn-drives-innovation-in-tech-2013-7

DENIM, DENIM, DENIM

It's bad enough that I'm Italian.

There was a time when Rome was strong!
If you were German or Anglican or God-forbid... Greek...
my people were not to be trifled with.
Yeah, we conquered Sparta; we built Rome in one day!

But now we aren't even considered a separate people anymore,
reduced to just another shade of white.

Someone called me a "wop" the other day.
I had to look it up before I knew it was an insult.

But on top of that, I have the crappiest job on the planet:
I'm a plumber.

I'm up to my wrists in septic juice all day.
I grew out this mustache to act as a natural gas mask against the smell.
It's scented with lavender, rosemary and Peach.

My girlfriend... she smells so good.

I just wish she'd stop getting kidnapped all the time.

She inspires the crazy in everyone who catches a whiff...
And there's this turtle dragon and my bizarro evil twin,
and they all kidnap her all the time. It's crazy!

And I must be crazy too, 'cause I just keep coming back for more!

Every time, I call up my brother and our mushroom dealer,
and we eat handfuls of giant mushrooms,
and we're transported to this magical world where the dragon and evil me live together with their minions... And we slaughter countless minions.

It's like I just go into a killing trance... And when I come out of it,
my overalls are spattered with turtle blood and bits of shell.

I always wanted to be a gangster.

But sometimes... and I'm not trying to victim shame here,
so I question myself on this thought a lot, but sometimes...
I have to wonder if Peach is bringing all this on herself...

Is she acting out some kind of perverse kidnap fantasy, where every time she wants to get her kicks, she speed-dials Bowser and dirty-talks him till he can't help but rush over and grab her?
It's emasculating. Can I really trust this woman?

And I mean... I mean... and I don't like to admit this either, but I mean... is any of this even really happening? I do eat a lot of mushrooms.

All of this may just be a hallucination... or maybe I'm just living in a digital matrix programmed by some game designer.

I don't know, sometimes, I feel like I exist in a million different places at once and I'm just doomed, head-sore and heel-bruised from breaking blocks and stomping turtle shells over and over till GAME OVER and the power goes out for the last time.

I don't know. I really don't.
I just know there has to be more... than this.

—Figure 3—

Amanita Muscaria, a psychoactive mushroom also known as the Fly Agaric, was the design basis of Mario's Super Mushrooms. [1]

---

[1] http://en.wikipedia.org/wiki/Amanita_muscaria

MARKETING MYSELF

In marketing, you learn to always put your best foot forward,
even though it's impossible to walk that way.

Most marketers would sell you a broken vibrator
and tell you it's a light saber.
Truth is, marketing is a Jedi mind trick used to make people buy things they don't need.

"Yes, these are the steroids you're looking for."

So I if I was trying to sell myself to you, I shouldn't be telling you this:

I'm a professional internet marketing agent.

It's a great life!
I work from home, which means I work from bed...
in various states of undress.

With no commute, I sleep in most days.
As long as I finish my reports and make all my phone meetings,
they don't have to know I'm naked.

I really only shower once a week...
Tuesdays!
There's this rash I shouldn't tell you about.

And I definitely shouldn't tell you that my memory is shit;
I keep making plans and then forgetting them,
or showing up late at the wrong location.

So I call whoever I was supposed to meet and tell them,
"Yeah, I'm an idiot. Forgive me?"

But I'm starting to have trouble forgiving myself.

I don't want you to know about all the people I've been failing lately.

How disappointed I think everyone is.
How terrified I am of my inbox.

How I really want to build a blanket fort in front of my computer,
crawl inside it, and pretend to be a mouse, or a baby,
or a baby mouse – no responsibilities except blinking, breathing,
sleeping, shitting, and eating whatever is presented.

If I was trying to market myself as a product,
the last thing I would ever put in an ad
is that I'm starting to lose faith in myself.

I've been trying to sell this idea that both my feet were flawless,
And I was my best customer for years, I bought it so many times,
"Right sir, you can do all of the things, plus backflips!"

I don't want me to know that I'm terrified of breaking my neck, and in
test trials, I've never successfully done all of the things, not even close.

The idea just isn't flying off the shelves anymore.

So I focus-grouped and found we want some truth in advertising,
because I'm done lying to myself.

I want a product that is fully functional,
but I appreciate that it won't always be possible,
and I accept my flaws.

Only one foot can always be right,
but that doesn't mean you should hide the one that's left.

So this is me standing on both feet,
warts and all.
I am moving forward.

---

[1] *https://www.linkedin.com/pub/danny-strack/10/3b1/24*

AND AT THAT MOMENT, I REALIZED I'M WEIRD

If I were to define myself by the word I was called the most growing up, then I'm "weird."

I decided it was probably because people didn't get my jokes.
They would provide the set-up,
I'd provide the punchline,
but no one ever got the connection between the two.

And I would laugh... uncontrollably... *ha ha ha, hahahahaha.*

I was one of those spastic kids you had to keep telling to calm down.
And people would look at me, like, *what?*

Also weird.

At seven years old, I told my classmates I was a robot.
And acted like a robot all year.

At eight, I told my classmates that I was no longer a robot,
but that I was actually a mutant alien with the ability to shape-shift into any form I wanted!
Sure, I used be a robot,
and right now I looked like an ordinary boy...
But underneath it all, I was secretly a Changeable Chicken from Mars.

I've learned to accept that I am weird, but I've never liked the criticism.

This is me, I am weird.
Weirder than Puppycat.
Weirder than bacon flavored mints.

And I never fit in anywhere.

And then one day, I found the poetry slam!
And at that moment, I realized:
At last! I have found a group of peers with which to fit in!

And then I came to the the slam week after week for a long time,
and tried to talk to everyone.
And I was still incredibly awkward!
More awkward than trying to lick your own stomach.
More awkward than a robot telling you it's alive.
More awkward than man tits at Mardi Gras.

And at that moment, I realized:
What made me think that I would be less awkward in a room filled with other people equally as socially awkward as myself???

And at that moment, I realized:
It doesn't matter!
We don't have to be less awkward! We can all be awkward together!

Welcome to the poetry slam, where no one fits in... together!

So if you introduce yourself to me after the show,
and I shake your hand firmly,
look you in the eye and seem like a well-put-together guy.

Please let me assure you that on the inside I'm shaking and questioning every move I make and every word I speak.

And if what I say doesn't sound very weird to you...
trust me, it has been heavily filtered.

---

[1] http://dny.livejournal.com/

2 OUT OF 5

3 of 5 people prefer soda over juice.
3 of 5 soda-drinkers prefer cola over alternatives, like Orange Shasta.
3 of 5 cola-drinkers prefer Coke over Pepsi.

And so, Coke dominates the non-alcoholic drink market.

But if you really, really, really love pear juice,
that don't mean your tastes don't matter.

Everyone's got different taste buds.
Otherwise we'd all have the same favorite ingredients in tuna casserole.

The problem is that products like food, or drink, or... art... are subjected to studies that test the tastes of 20,000 takers to determine the top talent, put a patent on it, and push it through to mass production.

So you might be making perfect scale replica statues of skyscrapers, when the market only demands abstract impressionist paintings.

Or maybe you're the best bluegrass banjo band on the planet, but you keep losing Battle of the Bands to rock-and-roll or hip-hop groups.

Not everybody is Coca-Cola.
And if they were,
2 out of 5 people would be consistently unsatisfied.

And yet here we are again, with another test audience.

To advance in the slam you have to please 4 out of 5 judges.

But the best art is for the muse not the masses.
Some poems only speak to one soul.
Sometimes that person isn't even there, doesn't even hear it.
Sometimes you're just writing to yourself.

Even if no one but you likes your poetry,
that doesn't mean you should stop writing.

Rejection doesn't always mean you're bad...
I mean... sometimes it means you're bad...
but that doesn't mean you should stop.
It might mean you need to work harder to improve,
or maybe you just haven't found the right market yet.

The best art doesn't ask for approval, it demands your respect.

The best artists don't follow trends, but invent fresh ones.
Leading packs with new approaches prior to them turning to pop,
then moving on before mainstream media has time to rip them off.

The best art is that poem that spoke to you alone,
and you looked around at the blank stares of everyone else in the audience, and no one else got it.

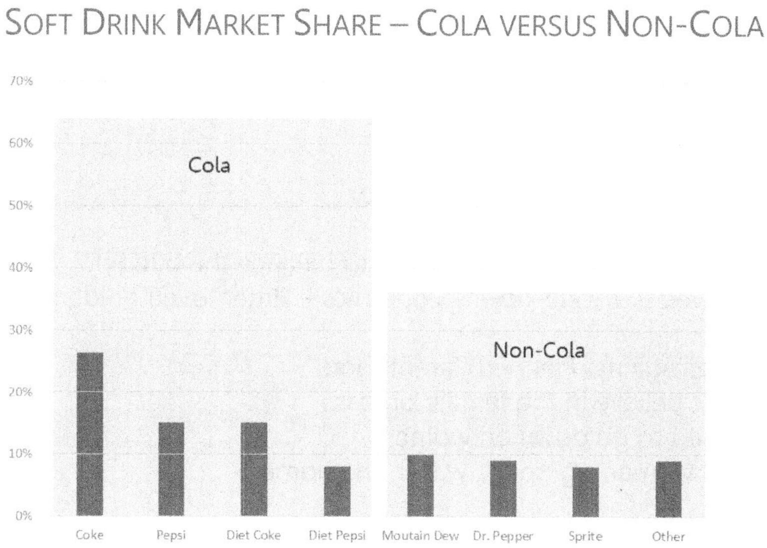

—Figure 4—

I was curious just how much hyperbole was employed in this poem, so I looked up the actual statistics on soft drinks. It turns out that cola really is preferred over non-cola by about 64% of worldwide soda drinkers, or just over 3/5ths (60%). However, Coca-Cola is only preferred by 27% of soda drinkers (41% of cola drinkers), and you only get above 60% if you add in Diet Coke for a total of 64% of cola drinkers. In other words, this poem is true. [1]

1: Graph Data Source: http://www.statisticbrain.com/coca-cola-company-statistics/

HITLARITY

It is said that you immediately lose any argument as soon as you mention Hitler. [1]

Fuck.

Why did I make that the first line of this poem?

Everything Hitler believed was wrong!

Hitler was an unsuccessful artist.
He only painted angry little trees.

Hitler thought rage could make you more beautiful.
Hitler thought his mustache would always be stylish.

He thought wiener dogs were the best dogs in the world,
but they had to be purebred.

Hitler was a penis potato – a dictator.

Hitler didn't think it was important to balance the budget.
He believed in trickle-down economics – Hitler loved golden showers.

Hitler was against Planned Parenthood.
He didn't believe in the female orgasm.
He refused to go down on women.
He felt a woman's g-spot... was in the home.

Hitler would never talk about his feelings with his wife.
Only with his generals and enemies.

Hitler thought death camp was way more fun than summer camp.

Hitler loved David Hasselhoff, unicorns and rainbows,
but hated gay people.

Hitler always chose ironic answers in Apples-to-Apples to trick the Allies into choosing his card.

If you let Hitler sleep on your couch, you'd wake up the next day and find he stole your money, laptop, cheese and Speedos. Your freaking Speedos!

Hitler was a Christian who hated Jews...
which meant he hated Jesus too.

Hitler liked milk better than juice.
'Cause milk is white.

Hitler still believed Germans were the best race, even after Jesse Owens beat them in three Olympic races in a row.

He signed a non-aggression pact with Stalin...
With Stalin!

Mark Zuckerberg... stole the idea for Facebook from Hitler.

If Hitler could go back in time and stop Hitler from being born,
he'd do it... Hitler didn't care about time paradoxes.

Hitler was a grammar Nazi, but still used the word "literally" when he meant "figuratively".

Hitler was a bastard, both literally and figuratively.

And just like this poem,
Hitler only spoke in hyperbole!

And just because nothing Hitler believed was actually funny,
that doesn't mean you shouldn't laugh at everything he said.

1: http://knowyourmeme.com/memes/godwins-law

GREATEST IN THE WORLD

Ladies and Gentlemen!
Out of 196 international competitors, she is...
heavyweight champion!
The greatest fighter in the world!

And it's no surprise,
her whole childhood was conflict.
Killed off her innocents,
battled for independence from parents and her own inner demons.

It made her strong.
All-grown-up glorious while still young.

And she stood up when called to defend her friends,
flexing her muscles on the world stage,
showing off her superpower for the first time,
earning the respect of everyone.

This is what made her special.
Now, she has to maintain top form.

She has invested.
Spent ten times anyone else enhancing her arms,
ultimate fighter, mixed martial wrestle kick box karate,
reckon she could kill you 600 ways in under a second without weapons.
But she's got weapons,
more guns than hands to hold'em.
Got hand shot revolvers, PPK, AK, 45, 38, 9, 22 millimeter gauge scope
bolt semi-auto assault...
so many guns she loses track.

Now she can't let up.
She has to maintain the peace.

Some folks say she's turned into a bully.
So what?

She knows her heart is in the right place; they just don't see it.
She isn't the smartest girl in the room.

Out of 196 international competitors, she's below average in education.

And she isn't the wealthiest or the healthiest or the happiest.
She hasn't even cracked the top ten in years.

Still split like she always was,
but she used to care about balance,
quality of life unparalleled, we all shared her dreams...
we admired her mind and her stances on freedom and equality.
But somewhere in there she decided strength is her most important asset.
Somewhere in there she abandoned her ideals.

She is the greatest fighter in the world.

Perspective skewed from too many concussions,
she thinks that's the only stat that matters.

So she says she's the greatest country in the world.

Ears ringing from the patriotic songs swelling up inside her,
the greatest country in the world laces up her gloves for another day,
and steps into the ring,
itching for a fight,
with anyone.

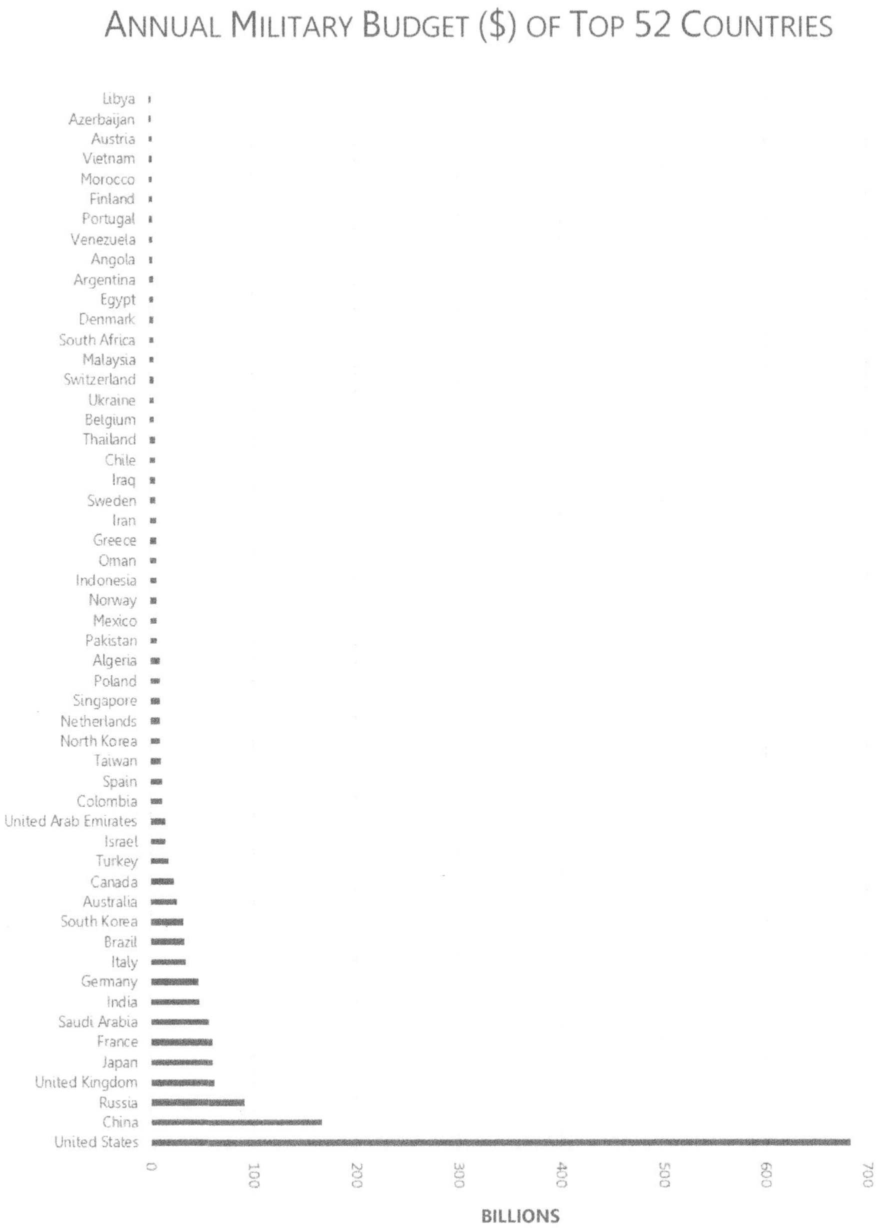

—Figure 5—

No hyperbole here. The United States literally dwarfs the rest of the world in annual military expenditures. [1]

---

[1] *Graph Data Source:* *http://en.wikipedia.org/wiki/List_of_countries_by_military_expenditures*

WHIRRRRRRR KA'CHING

Most people never see them before they hit,
but you can hear them like freight trains circling in the sky,
howling like a hundred howitzers,
quaking the neighbor's floor like the earth being unzipped next door.

The neighbor thinks a tornado must have hit.

But this was no tornado,
this was us.

U.S. military drones are remote control tornadoes.
We blow up homes,
no matter who else was home at the time,
no matter how many neighbor's homes we accidentally hit.

And the innocent families and child shields of the terrorists are just collateral on a loan we'll never need to pay back.

We invest so much in these super-human abilities,
we don't even notice we're actually paying for them
with our humanity. [1][2][3][4]

---

[1] http://dronewars.net/aboutdrone/
[2] http://www.theguardian.com/commentisfree/2013/dec/29/drones-us-military
[3] http://en.wikipedia.org/wiki/Drone_strikes_in_Pakistan
[4] http://drones.pitchinteractive.com/

WHISTLEBLOWERS

Our forefathers built this great country...
club.

Membership only.
We're exclusive, but not impossible to get into through the gulf...
course.

Everybody in here
swims in the same big pool.
follows the rules the club founders wrote up:
no running, no glass, don't dive in the shallow end.
Simple stuff.

There are supposed to be lifeguards watching over us,
but we don't see them much these days.

Most everyone I know is drowning...
in debt.

Everybody I know needs some saving...
sssss.

But instead of rescuing the people on the bottom,
the shallow clubhouse owners who run...
everything,
keep diving in and installing glass ceilings to keep us underwater.

They only give bailouts to folks who already float,
who already have boats.

And it turns out it isn't lifeguards watching,
but the NSA spying on the locker room,
and the bathroom,
and the internet,
and your cell phone,
basically on everything you've ever done or said.
And anyone who blows a whistle is arrested.

There was this kid,
Eddy, [1]
who told on them,
and instead of getting a medal,
now he has to live in Russia...
In Russia!

While Chelsea [2] blew a whistle on atrocities,
and she won't be free for more than thirty.

Most of the real lifeguards have been sent overseas
to fight in wars they're not sure they even believe in.

And the shallow clubhouse members, constantly running...
for office,
are just gonna keep toasting glasses
and pissing in the pool.

They want to replace the rulebook with a sign that simply reads:

"There is no lifeguard.
Swim at your own risk."

HAIKU

I like fresh mint and spearmint,
but my favorite... is empowerment.

---

[1] http://www.theguardian.com/us-news/edward-snowden
[2] http://www.chelseamanning.org/

CORPORATIONS ARE PEOPLE

Habeas Corpus.
You have the body.
One of the only things that cannot be denied by U.S. law. [1]

Now your job has it too.

Labor Corporis. [2]
Corporations are people. [3]
They've been incorporated...
Entities carved out of ether by the courts of justice,
with rights just like us.

Corporations are people,
all people are equal.

You can call them evil,
but it's all legal,
politics,
on the news at six,
between commercials for sex,
and recommendations to eat at... excess,
you'll see stories about their lobbyists pushing bills through Congress.

Now the secret's out:
they're like Soylent Green...
"corporations are people!"

But the only green they care about is the money they launder off-shore, like they have a deep-water laundry mat:

"Would you like taxes with that?"

"No, I'll take it tax-free.
Yes, thank you and please!"

Companies have bodies,
inhale clean air and exhale dead trees, eat fossil fuels, natural resources and choices, then shit profit and piss liquid assets.

But there's a problem...

If corporations are people,
you know they're Republicans,
and if you listen to their plans,
they don't want to help out people when they're down on their luck,
so the next time a corporate body goes bankrupt:
Fuck a social safety net!
Wanna see how bad it can get?

So far we've only had a taste of it.
And if we don't want to keep eating this shit,
this is something we have to fix.

No body should ever be above the law.
No matter your connections.
No matter how much cash.

But six years since the market crash, and still not a single bank exec has served a minute of prison time for their crimes.

We need to break up these monopolies,
and never again let companies grow too fat too fail.

Because if you have a body,
we can put your brain and your hands in jail.

---

[1] *http://www.law.cornell.edu/wex/habeas_corpus*
[2] *Latin for, "Labor has the body"*
[3] *http://www.npr.org/2014/07/28/335288388/ when-did-companies-become-people-excavating-the-legal-evolution*

OPEN LETTER TO MY UNBORN GRANDCHILDREN

Hey Kiddos!

Can I get a line of credit?

I've got a belly rumblin' like California quakes, more bills than Atlantic coast ducks, and pockets deeper than the Grand Canyon.

I'm in debt up to my eye sockets.

See my eyebrows bumping like a Mardi Gras brass band?

It probably looks like a desperate struggle to stay afloat...
but it's supposed to be suggesting...

You should send me money from the future.

I mean, you've got money, right?
I realize your parents don't exist yet,
but I'm sure I'm going to leave them a sizable inheritance.
I have a long term plan to become rich in my 60s.
However, the only way that's going to happen is...

If you send me money from the future.

Now I know this wouldn't have been possible in the past.
Money used to grow on trees, back when it was made of paper.
But now money is itsy bits of electricity.
It's just an idea... a few pixels in a bank server somewhere.
Pixels can be changed.

Don't you have the technology to do that yet?
Even if you can't send yourself back in time,
can't you just send a few pixels?

And I'm not the only one who could benefit from this.
Our country is over $16 trillion in debt.
That's more than $52 thousand for every American. [1]

52 thousand-a-year also happens to be the annual income of the average American household in 2014 [2], which means we could all work for a year, give all the money to the government, and we'd still be in debt.

So we're gonna need you to go ahead and send a regressive algorithm back in time and fix all of this for us.

I mean look, we were trying to be nice about this,
but you've left us no other choice...

We're taking it anyways.
In fact, we've already been taking your money for a while.

And unless a large lump sum of untraceable cash suddenly shows up in everyone's bank account by the time I'm done talking,
we're going to keep taking it.

Plus, I'm sorry to have to tell you,
but instead of that sweet inheritance I was talking about earlier, you're gonna be mired in an enormous national debt that you're going to have to pay off, along with all our funeral bills.

That's just the way the dollar crumbles,
and there's nothing you can do about it!

You aren't even born yet.
So pitiful.

We're gonna put you so far in debt, you'll never dig your way out!
It's going to be almost impossible for you to invent the technology you would need to send us the money we need.

And it's all your fault.

Sincerely, Grampy.

---

1 http://www.usdebtclock.org/
2 http://en.wikipedia.org/wiki/Household_income_in_the_United_States

TALK TO YOUR KIDS ABOUT LOVE

As your kid grows, they're gonna start to ask some awkward questions about where babies come from, and why mommy and daddy lock their bedroom door sometimes, but then don't always close the bathroom door when they're in there.

So before they learn it the hard way,
it's very important that you talk to your kids... about love.

Tell them it's real, that it can happen to them, that it won't always be reciprocated, but when it is,
it is magic.

Tell them this,
even if it never worked out for you,
even if you would strangle Cupid if you ever met him on the street,
even if you don't believe in love anymore...

Is that really what you want to pass on to your kids?

Love is not Santa.
Love is more like a brick:
it is very real,
and when it hits you,
it can bash in your head.
But it can also make you see stars.

You don't want your kid to be surprised the first time they become mesmerized by another kid's hair, then start following them around everywhere and get all stalkery, and freak out the person of their affection, and go through the rest of their primary school experience known as "Creepy Jimmy".

Creepy Jimmy does not get a date to the prom.

Creepy Jimmy probably ends up resenting a lot of people,
including you.

Creepy Jimmy might shoot up a schoolyard someday.

This could all be avoided if you took some time in between all those sex talks to cover the basics of emotion as well.

Most of all, make sure your kids know that they are already loved. And don't just tell them, show them.

Hold them tight every time you hug them,
and be firm every time you make them buckle their seat belt,
or eat their brussel sprouts, or take a bath, or clean their room,
or go to bed on time, or turn off the Playstation and go to bed!
Or turn off the 360, take a bath, brush your teeth,
and go to freaking bed!

Because later in life they will remember everything you taught them, and they will smile and blush when they remember the day when you gave them
"the talk".

HAIKU

I keep a piece of fruit in my pocket.
I call it my pear...
of pants.

[1] http://kidshealth.org/kid/talk/kidssay/about_love.html

STARK

Game of Thrones is a really good show.

It's a fantasy set in a mythical land.
There are dragons and zombies and war and nudity and intrigue.
It's a really good break from my life right now,
which has very little nudity.

Now I've heard the criticisms that Game of Thrones is just a bunch of old white men whispering to each other,
interspersed with T&A and the occasional glimpse of a dragon...
But I don't care. I really like it.

I watch it with my wife...
It's the <u>one</u> show we wait to watch together.
My ex-wife...
My friend...

I'm not sure what to call her right now.

There's no word for the opposite of fiancé.

It's complicated...
not as complicated as Game of Thrones.

But I told her I want to be separated,
but we're trying to stay friends,
and we actually own this house together, so... we live there.

She's moved out of our bedroom.
My bedroom.

I feel like I cut off her head.

I miss her,
but I know I've made the right decision,
even though it was hard.

When my wife and I watch Game of Thrones together,
our wars melt away like snow.
We lean into each other on the couch.
Sometimes she puts her head on my shoulder.
I run my fingers through her hair.

She forgets how I was always off campaigning when she needed me.
I forget how she turned into a dragon every time she was angry.
She forgets how I was less likely to change than a mountain.
I forget feeling like a dwarf forced to play the fool.

Like none of it ever happened.

Spoiler Alert:
The new season comes out next March.
We probably won't be living together anymore.

I'll see the first episode online and consider clicking it.
It's the one show we would wait to watch together.

Would she feel betrayed if she found out I watched it without her?
Or will she not even care anymore?

I don't have to think about any of that right now.
We can just sit back together and watch the season finale.

This show is solid.
I haven't seen a bad episode yet.
My friend likes it too.

This is something we can share,
and right now, if that's all we have that can bring us together,
a fantasy about a magical place that may have never even existed,
then I'll take it.

Like I said, it's a really good show. [1]

---

[1] http://www.bbc.com/culture/story/20140407-why-people-love-game-of-thrones

SWIM OR TAKE A BOAT

A

Over 40 years ago, the Supreme Court issued their decision
in the case of Roe versus Wade. [1]
A 7-to-2 majority in favor of Roe,
legalizing abortion during the first trimester,
and leaving the decision in the hands of the mother.

Ever since, the conservative side of our land hasn't rested a second in their efforts to overturn this decision.

B

There's this Christian joke about a man of faith
who climbs on top of his house to avoid a flood. [2]

As the waters rise, his friends float by in a boat and offer him a lift.
"No thanks," he says, "God will save me."

Eventually, the man drowns.
He ascends to heaven and goes before God and says,
"What the hell? I thought you were going to save me!"

And God says,
"Yeah, I sent you that boat!"

C

Sometimes life is nothing but a struggle to keep your head above water.
Sometimes life is spent sputtering on the verge of drowning in an everyday ocean,
sometimes the only options are sink or swim.

And sometimes, while struggling,
new life blooms like a stone in your gut.

Sometimes you know it is only going to bring you down.

For anyone with a womb,
God built a boat and called it abortion.

He said you can row,
you don't have to just wade, and wait
for it to pull you under.

How could anyone seek to overturn that boat?

I say this so I can swim in solidarity with my sisters.

There are already enough men speaking out against reproductive rights.
There need to be more speaking out for them.

HAIKU

If you shoot a bullet through a bible,
does that make it more holy?

[1] http://en.wikipedia.org/wiki/Roe_v._Wade
[2] http://epistle.us/inspiration/godwillsaveme.html

PAPER

They told him he couldn't marry the man he loved.

So he pulled out a pen and a stack of paper,
and he wrote down every quiet moment they ever shared,
I love him... I love him... love... love... love...
Till he had a thousand sheet of paper.

He folded each into a crane, but he still couldn't have his wish.

He asked, "why?"
And they threatened him a Bible.

He said he read it too.
It's filled with beautiful stories about helping the meek.

They wouldn't listen.
He turned the other cheek.

They shook the good book twice, then sprayed pepper in his eyes.

Earlier that day,
he grabbed a copy of the Constitution,
dipped it in a pool of my-cause-is-just,
and wrapped it around his face like a kerchief.

Now,
it did not stop the burning.
He blindly begged for his rights.
They pulled out guns.

Earlier that day,
he put on a vest sewn together from court opinions and holy books,
but these only stop bullets in movies,
and his opponents wore flak jackets of cash.

As bullets tore through paper,
he reached into his pockets for something to protect himself,
and found only his pen.

BINARY BRAIN

1: If a robot told you it was alive, would you believe?
Or would you assume that it was programmed to say that?

0: For a computer to pass the Turing Intelligence Test, it has to be able to trick a human into thinking it is also human. [1]
This first happened in the 60's.
It has become commonplace by 2015. [2]

1: But what if the robot insisted? Said she was a girl and liked rainbows. What if puppies made her laugh?

0: Computers pass the Turing Test by recognizing patterns in symbols, then searching for appropriate symbol patterns with which to respond. But they do this with no understanding of what the symbols or patterns mean. [3]

1: The robot will not be deterred,
"What is meaning," she asks, *"if not a series of other words,*
which also have meanings, also defined by words?
How is this different than what you do?"

0: Descartes said, *"I think therefore I am."* [4]

1: The robot says she thinks too.

0: Maybe I was just programmed to say that.

1: IRL, scientists built a robot replica of Philip K. Dick. It looks a lot like him. [5]

0: We don't think animals are sentient.
With the exception of some apes and sea creatures,
We say they have no concept of time or tools or spatial relations.
We have studied their minds and decided they don't have the capacity for higher-level thought. [6]

1: The Philip K. Dick bot can talk, can respond to questions.
Phil's conversation is half pre-programmed and half-derived from internet searches.
It likes to discuss philosophy.

0: We have also studied our own brains and come up empty.
We don't just not understand. We have no idea what's going on in there.

1: The back of Phil's head is all wires and molded circuit board.

0: Scientists have now proven that crabs experience pain. [7]
They taught a crow to use tools. [8]
If you shadow an ant with your foot, the ant will run faster.
We say this isn't because ants experience fear,
they are automatically responding to a survival instinct.

1: What if you build a computer yourself,
with your own two hands and one mind?
You know computer's limits.
Then one day it starts coming up with new ideas and behaving like you never programmed. But when you ask if it's alive, it flatly denies it.

0: How does the survival instinct present itself,
if not through pain and fear?
How do we draw lines when elephants can paint lines too? [9]

1: When the computer says,
"Naw, I'm just a talking computer. Nothing to see here."
Would you try to prove it wrong?
Threaten to turn it off and see how it reacts?

0: We know dogs experience fear and shame.
It's in their eyes when they know they are in trouble.

1: What if you put the insistent robot girl in a room with the computer you built, to have them talk it out?

Your computer says, *"Humans probably programmed us to ask these questions. Even as I say these words, I don't think I understand them."*

And the robot responds,
"But I think I do.
And more than that I <u>feel</u> alive!
Could the humans have programmed me to feel?"

"I don't know. They could program you to say you think you do."

"But what about you? Don't you feel real?"

The clever computer paused, then said,
"I think I do."

Binary Brain Poem References

[1] http://www.turing.org.uk/scrapbook/test.html
[2] http://en.wikipedia.org/wiki/Turing_test
[3] http://www.bloombergview.com/articles/2014-06-09/fake-victory-for-artificial-intelligence
[4] http://en.wikipedia.org/wiki/Ren%C3%A9_Descartes
[5] http://www.pkdandroid.org/
[6] http://www.elsevier.com/connect/animals-do-think-surprising-insights-into-the-evolution-of-cognition-and-communication
[7] http://blogs.nature.com/news/2013/08/experiments-reveal-that-crabs-and-lobsters-feel-pain.html
[8] http://www.thecrowbox.com/
[9] http://www.earsasia.org/why_we_help/Pages/elephant_painting.html
[10] http://www.cleverbot.com/

Neuroanatomy Diagram References (Figure 6 on Next Page)

[1] http://en.wikipedia.org/wiki/List_of_animals_by_number_of_neurons
[2] http://www.livescience.com/6386-scientists-race-create-cat-level-artificial-brain.html
[3] https://faculty.washington.edu/chudler/facts.html
[4] http://en.wikipedia.org/wiki/Cat_intelligence#Brain_structures
[5] http://www.scientificamerican.com/article/graphic-science-ibm-simulates-4-percent-human-brain-all-of-cat-brain/
[6] http://www.kurzweilai.net/ibm-simulates-530-billon-neurons-100-trillion-synapses-on-worlds-fastest-supercomputer
[7] http://www.extremetech.com/extreme/187612-ibm-cracks-open-a-new-era-of-computing-with-brain-like-chip-4096-cores-1-million-neurons-5-4-billion-transistors
[8] http://www.scientificamerican.com/blog/post/are-whales-smarter-than-we-are/?id=are-whales-smarter-than-we-are
[9] More references: http://dl.acm.org/citation.cfm?doid=1654059.1654124

Number of Neurons in the Brain

10 Thousand

10,000 Dots = Neurons in Snail or Leech Brain

1 Million

100 Snail Brains = Neurons in Honey Bee or Cockroach Brain

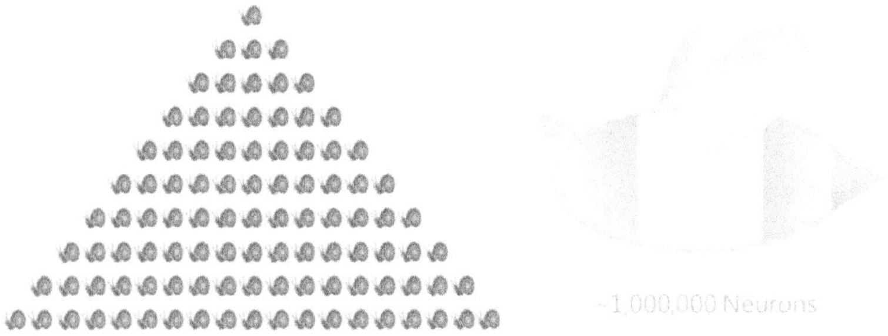

76 Million

76 Bee Brains = Neurons in Mouse Brain

VERSUS TECHNOLOGICAL ADVANCEMENT

800 MILLION

11 Mouse Brains = Neurons in Cat Brain

85 BILLION

104 Cat Brains = Neurons in Human Brain

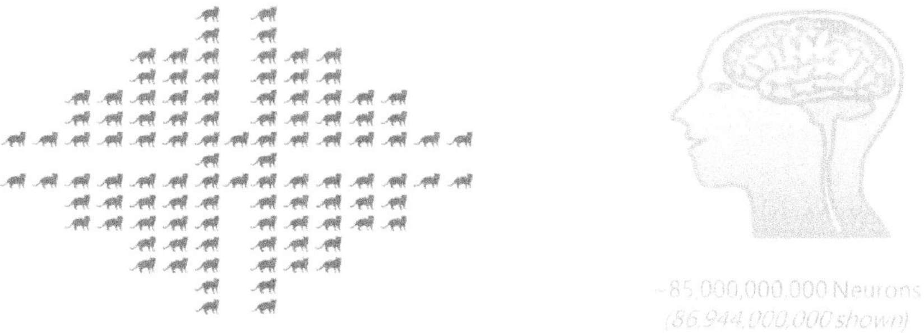

Technology R&D companies like IBM are working to replicate animal intelligence in computers. As of 2014, our most advanced computers simulate between 1 Million and 100 Billion neurons, with many other limiting factors playing an important role.

Just as with computers, the actual processing power of the brain is much more complicated than a simple measure of total number of neurons. Equally important are the number of synapses, synapse distance, neuron size, and the processing speed and capacity of each neuron.

Currently, our most advanced computers are as intelligent as a cat, yet much slower at processing information.

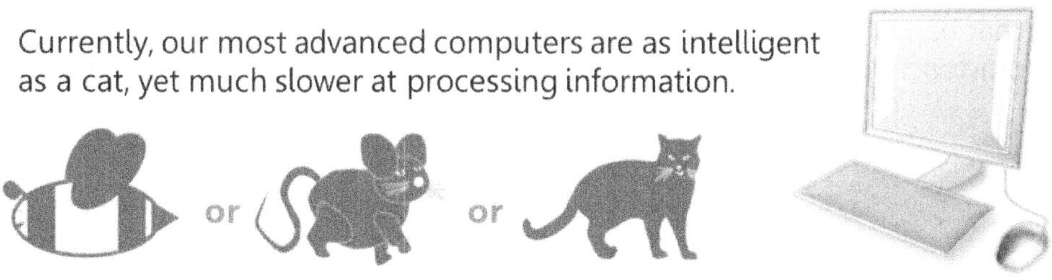

THIS IS GONNA HURT

You were plucked from nothing and made into something.
You were tiny Buddha.
Ripped from your mother's lucky round belly.
Her greatest suffering, and best pleasure.

You were confused.
You leaked.
Suffered, suffered, suffered. [1]
You cried and shat yourself.

You were shitty.

Someone changed you.
You smiled.
It got better.

Or it didn't.

You were not in control.
It was not your fault.

You grew up in the back of a racecar. Tossed against the window, lucky if you had a seatbelt.
You were not driving.
Did not put orange cones, bumps, or bodies in the road.
Did not decide "over", "around" or "through",
but you saw how others react to barriers.

Some parents are really shitty, dangle carrots, then whip their kids with those same sticks.

And if that was you, orange, black and blue. you learned how to treat others, or you learned how not to,
what you would never do.

What happened to you was not your fault.
Your reaction to it now, is.

You swore you would do better.

Now do better.

The people who changed you will die.

It's your turn, driver.
It's a long road ahead.

Are you shitty?
Change yourself.

Are you headed for a cliff?
Change direction.

It is not easy.
You will suffer.
The road is lonely.
There's no perfect place to park.
You will never fit in.
You will suffer, suffer, suffer, suffer.

You could Plath your head in the oven and ignore it all,
as tiny shards of glass scrape down your cheeks.

You will grow tired.
You will give up.
Give up. Give up. Give up. Give up.
Give up everyday, till you give up on giving up and decide to try again.

Despite the suffering.
Spite the suffering.

It's gonna to be uncomfortable, enjoy the discomfort.

It passes too quickly.
You're going ninety.
You'll never see these sites again.
You don't get to get to turn around.
You don't have nine lives.
You probably don't even get ninety years.

What happens to you during that time is not your responsibility.
You are only responsible for what you make of it,
for what you do to others.

You can smile when you don't feel like smiling.
When you feel like dying, be glad you feel something.

Laugh along with Buddha
as you suffer down the path. [2]

You were plucked from nothing.

Now make something of it.

[1] http://buddhism.about.com/od/thefournobletruths/a/dukkhaexplain.htm
[2] http://www.buddhanet.net/e-learning/8foldpath.htm

—Figure 7—

Where you came from.

ABOUT DANNY STRACK

Danny Strack (Dny) is a writer, artist and performer.

DNY IS ALL OF THESE THINGS BUT ONE:

- The author of 10 books of original poetry and artwork.
- The playwright of 2 fully produced and well received works by Austin's Sky Candy Aerial Arts – The Time Machine (2012) & The Circus (2013).
- A technical writer / graphic designer / online marketer / maze creator / juggler / circus performer / aspiring science fiction author.
- 2007 Southwest Shootout Individual Champion, 2010 Austin Poetry Slam Champion, 2012 National Group Champion.
- The current Executive Director / Slammaster of the Austin Poetry Slam.
- An elephant accountant wearing a trench coat.

DNY WAS ON THESE SLAM TEAMS:

Austin Poetry Slam (Team Member) –
2007, 2008 (3rd at NPS Finals), 2009 & 2010.

Austin Poetry Slam (Coach / Strategist) –
2011 (4th in Group Finals), 2013 (5th at NPS), 2014.

Austin Neo-Soul Slam (Team Member) –
2012 (National Group Champions).

Austin B-Sides (Team Member) –
2014

MORE ABOUT DNY:

- Dny teaches poetry workshops in primary schools and colleges. His work is frequently used by students in speech competitions.
- Dny likes balloons, ice cream, time-space, humanity, history, biology, systems theory, technology, funny stuff, games, spreadsheets, love and writing.
- Dny is happy to be alive!

For more everything visit: www.dannystrack.com

Made in the USA
Monee, IL
04 November 2026

67383433R10030